READING

SEAHORSE CONNECTIONS

# HELPING MY CHILD

A Guide to Supporting Reading

GRADE 2

SEAHORSE PUBLISHING

# TABLE OF CONTENTS

# THE SCIENCE OF READING

Reading is an essential skill for success in school and in life. In order to understand how children learn to read, parents should understand the science of reading.

The *science of reading* is a term that refers to more than 20 years of research by experts on how people learn to read. The research shows that reading does not come naturally. For many people, it takes significant effort. Learning how to read is most effective when it happens in a step-by-step process that is based on proven, research-supported strategies and techniques.

Good reading instruction has several important parts. It helps students develop skills in phonological awareness, phonics, fluency, vocabulary, and comprehension. All these skills help students build pathways in their brains that connect speech sounds to print and that connect words with their meanings. By using the science of reading as a guide, parents and teachers can support our children in learning how to read.

## KEYS TO EFFECTIVE READING INSTRUCTION

**Phonological Awareness:** The ability to notice, think about, and work with the sounds that make up spoken words

**Phonics:** Understanding the relationship between sounds and the letters that represent them in written words

**Fluency:** The ability to read quickly and accurately

**Vocabulary:** Understanding word meanings

**Comprehension:** Gaining meaning from reading

# CREATING SKILLED READERS

Reading is more than just sounding out words. Skilled readers are able to recognize words as well as understand their meanings on a deep level. They weave together memorization skills, phonics skills, vocabulary skills, background knowledge, and more.

## SCARBOROUGH'S READING ROPE

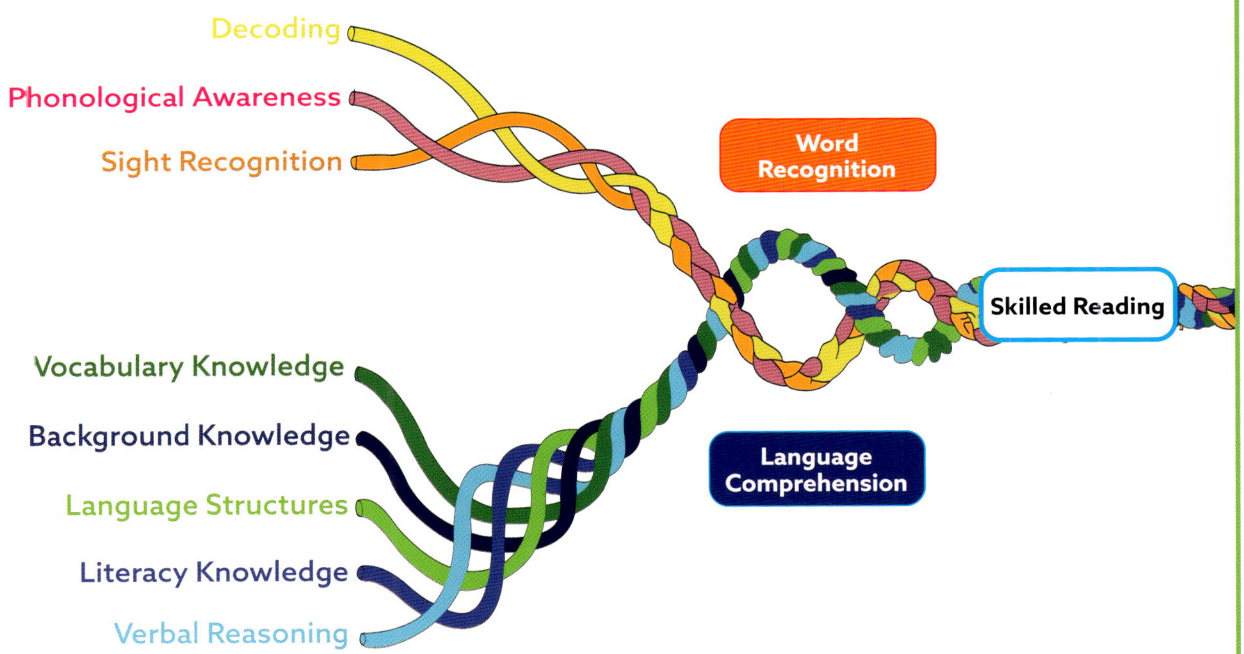


To show how children draw on a variety of abilities to become skilled readers, Dr. Hollis Scarborough created the Reading Rope. In 2001, this model was published in the *Handbook of Early Literacy Research* (Neuman/Dickinson).

# PHONOLOGICAL AND PHONEMIC AWARENESS: HEARING SOUNDS IN WORDS

Phonological awareness and phonemic awareness are important pre-reading skills. They describe a child's ability to hear, identify, and play with sounds in spoken language. These skills form an essential foundation for reading and writing development in second grade and beyond.

Children demonstrate phonological awareness when they recognize and manipulate, or change, parts of spoken words. Phonemic awareness is the last phonological awareness skill to develop. Children who have mastered phonemic awareness can hear, recognize, and play with the individual sounds, or phonemes, in spoken words.

## PHONOLOGICAL AWARENESS MILESTONES

| | |
|---|---|
| **Ages 3 to 4** | Produces real and pretend rhyming words |
| **Ages 4 to 5** | Claps or taps out syllables in words<br>Recognizes words that begin with the same sound<br>Segments or separates out each sound in words with three sounds<br>Blends or combines individual sounds to produce words that have three sounds<br>Counts the number of sounds in words that have three sounds |
| **Ages 5 to 6** | Segments or separates out each sound in words with four sounds<br>Identifies the first and last sounds in a word<br>Groups words with the same beginning sound<br>Identifies which word does not rhyme in a set of three words<br>Identifies which word is not the same in a set of three words |
| **Ages 6 to 7** | Deletes syllables from words when asked<br>Deletes sounds from words when asked<br>Substitutes syllables in words when asked<br>Substitutes sounds in words when asked |
| **Ages 7 to 8** | Uses phonological awareness skills to spell words |

# ACTIVITIES FOR BUILDING PHONOLOGICAL AWARENESS

## SYLLABLE HUNT

Look around the house to find things whose names have more than one syllable. Say the word and hold up a finger for each word part. For example, say, "bed-room" for bedroom and "ma-ca-ro-ni" for macaroni.

## SWITCH IT

Think of a one-syllable word. Ask your child to change the beginning, middle, or ending sound in the word to make a new word. Use this example, reading letters shown in between slash marks as sounds.

**Parent:** Change the /st/ sound in *stop* to /sh/. What is the new word?

**Child:** Shop.

**Parent:** Great job! Now, change the /ō/ sound in *float* to /ă/. What is the new word?

**Child:** Flat.

**Parent:** Excellent thinking. Try changing the /nk/ sound in *sink* to /ng/. What is the new word?

**Child:** Sing.

**Parent:** Terrific! You did it!

## WORD MAGIC GAME

The adult says a word. The child changes the beginning, middle, or ending sound to make a new word and says what changed. The adult changes the beginning, middle, or ending sound of the child's word to make a new word and says what changed. Keep going back and forth. How far can you go? Use this example, reading letters shown between slash marks as sounds.

**Parent:** Mop.

**Child:** Top. I changed /m/ to /t/.

**Parent:** Stop. I changed /t/ to /st/.

**Child:** Step. I changed /ŏ/ to /ĕ/.

**Parent:** Stem. I changed /p/ to /m/.

**Child:** Them. I changed /st/ to /th/.

**Parent:** Hmm. I can't think of a change that makes a real word. You win!

# PHONICS: LETTERS MAKE SOUNDS

Phonics is the knowledge that letters and combinations of letters represent sounds. This is an essential skill for beginning readers. Children who have the benefit of phonics instruction become better readers and spellers.

All words are made up of sounds. The word *dog* has three sounds. Each letter stands for one sound. The word *light* has three sounds. The letters *igh* represent one sound. The English language uses 44 sounds to make all words. However, there are only 26 letters in the alphabet. Some letters can make more than one sound. Other letters combine to make new sounds. This is like a code that beginning readers must figure out.

### PHONICS BENEFITS

- Improved reading ability
- Faster ability to match sounds to letters
- Easier time sounding out unknown words
- Reading level increases faster

## PHONICS 101

### CONSONANT OR VOWEL?

Consonant letters are *b, c, d, f, g, h, j, k, l, m, n, p, q, r, s, t, v, w, x, y* (as in *you*), and *z*.

Vowel letters are *a, e, i, o, u*, and *y* (as in *my* and *baby*). Short vowels are marked with a curved symbol, like a smile on top: /ă/. Long vowels are marked with a horizontal line on top: /ā/.

## ACTIVITIES FOR BUILDING PHONICS SKILLS

### SHAVING CREAM LETTERS

Squirt shaving cream onto a large baking sheet. Spread it around evenly. Choose a letter or group of letters that makes a single sound. Say the sound. Use a finger to write the letter in the shaving cream and say its name. Say the sound the letter makes as you underline it. You can also do this with whipped cream!

## SHORT VOWELS IN ACTION

Help your child remember short vowel sounds by associating an action with each one.

**A:** Pretend to bite an apple. Say, "I see a worm in my apple! Aaaah! Short *a* says /ă/ like what we said when we saw a worm in our apple!"

**E:** Slide your finger back and forth along the edge of a table. Say, "Eh-eh-edge. Short *e* says /ĕ/ like the beginning sound in *edge*."

**I:** Scratch your nose. Say, "I have an ih-ih-itch. Short *i* says /ĭ/ like the beginning sound in *itch*."

**O:** Open your mouth as if the doctor is checking your throat. Say, "Ahhhh. Short *o* says /ŏ/ like the sound you make at the doctor."

**U:** Point upward. Say, "Uh-uh-up. Short *u* says /ŭ/ like the beginning sound in *up*."

## KEEP IT SHORT

To avoid confusing beginning readers, don't add a vowel sound when you make consonant sounds. For example, the sound for letter *t* is /t/, not /tuh/.

## RAINBOW LETTERS

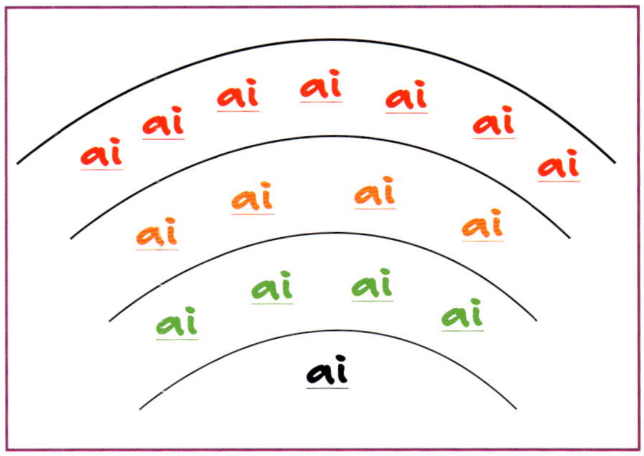


Draw a set of rainbow arches with space in between. Under the rainbow, write a letter or group of letters that makes one sound. Then, begin with the top arch. Use a red marker or crayon.

Follow these steps:

1. Say the sound the letter or letters make.
2. Write the letter or letters and say their names as you write.
3. Underline the letter or group of letters and say the sound it makes.

Repeat until the first arch is filled. Then, use an orange marker or crayon to fill the second arch in the same way as you say, write and spell, underline and read. Repeat for the next arches using different colors.

### Sound Sort

On individual index cards, write letters or groups of letters that make one sound. Sort them into groups such as long a sound, long e sound, long i sound, long o sound, long u sound, or special vowel sound. Are there other ways to categorize the cards?

# DECODING: SOUNDS MAKE WORDS

Decoding is the ability to sound out written words. Children use their knowledge of the phonics code to figure out words. A child with strong word decoding skills will have better reading comprehension skills.

When your child can see a word, understand the sound each letter represents, and blend sounds together to say the word, they are decoding. Once they can decode words independently, they have the tools they need to begin reading with fluency and comprehension.

## SOUNDING OUT WORDS

**Segmentation** means breaking a word into its individual sounds.

**dog:** /d/ /ŏ/ /g/ **sheep:** /sh/ /ē/ /p/

**Blending** means putting the sounds in a word together without pauses. Try these techniques to help your child with blending.

Continuous Blending: Stretch out each sound so that it continues into the next. Use your finger to slide across each letter from left to right.
**sip:** sssssssssssiiiiiiiiiip

Final Blending: Blend the first sounds together and then add the final sound.
**sip:** si–p

Isolated Blending: Say the first sound the loudest and then say each following sound softer. The last sound will be the softest.
**sip:** S i p

# ACTIVITIES FOR BUILDING DECODING SKILLS

## HIGHLIGHT IT

Use two different colors to highlight the consonant letters and vowel letters in a list of words.

**green** **think**

## MARK IT

In a list of words, mark vowel letters *v* and consonant letters *c*. Underline any letters that go together (vowel teams, consonant blends, consonant teams, etc.).

**gr ee n** **th i nk**
c c v v c c c v c c

## BOX IT

In a list of words, draw boxes around letters that go together.

**gr ee n** **th i nk**

## MAGIC E RAINBOW

Some words have the pattern vowel-consonant-*e*. The final *e* is called magic *e*, bossy *e*, or silent *e*. The vowel is long and says its name. Use this strategy for remembering the rule.

1. Write *v* under the vowel and *c* under the consonant that follows it.

   **game**
   v c

2. Cross out *e*. Draw an arch to connect *e* to the vowel. Say, "*E* makes the [vowel name] say [vowel name]." Example: "*E* makes the *a* say *a*."

   **game**
   v c

3. Sound out the word: /g/ /ā/ /m/.

# SIGHT WORDS AND HIGH-FREQUENCY WORDS: BUILDING BLOCKS FOR SUCCESS

Knowing sight words and high-frequency words helps create a strong foundation for beginning readers. Both types of words are often used in reading and writing. A sight word is a word that does not follow the regular rules of phonics and spelling. It is not decodable or is very difficult to decode. High-frequency words are decodable words that students need to know in order to be fluent readers. However, the phonics rules needed to decode them might not have been taught yet.

The word *like* is a high-frequency word. It can be decoded using the "magic *e*" or "bossy *e*" rule. Children who are just learning to read words such as *cat* and *sit* have not been taught this rule. However, since *like* is used in many simple stories, it is often introduced as a high-frequency word.

The word *have* is a sight word. It occurs often, but it does not follow the "magic *e*" or "bossy *e*" rule. Therefore, this word must be memorized, or identified by sight.

## GETTING UNSTUCK

What to do when your child gets stuck reading a word, or when they decode a word incorrectly? Allow time for your child to figure it out. Gently offer these strategies.

- Spell the word.
- Ask, "Do you see any letters that go together?"
- Ask, "Do you see any little words inside the longer word?"
- Say, "Let's sound out each part."

## SMALL BUT MIGHTY

Just 13 words make up 25 percent of all English words in print.

| | |
|---|---|
| a | of |
| and | that |
| for | the |
| he | to |
| in | was |
| is | you |
| it | |

# ACTIVITIES FOR LEARNING SIGHT WORDS AND HIGH-FREQUENCY WORDS

## Slap It!

Choose five words to learn. Write each on a sticky note. Place the notes around the house. When your child finds a word, have them read the word and then use their hand to slap it.

## COLORFUL WORDS

Write a word in the middle of a sheet of paper. Have your child choose a colored marker or pencil. Read the word. Have your child write the word in color, saying the name of each letter aloud as it is written. Underline the word from left to right while reading the word. Then, choose a new color and repeat. Keep choosing new colors until you have filled the page.

## Trace It

Write words on index cards. Have your child read each word aloud. Ask your child to use their index finger to trace each letter while saying its name. Then, use a finger to underline the word from left to right while reading the word. Repeat with the next card.

# WORD ATTACK SKILLS: WORDS HAVE PARTS

Skilled readers can look at unfamiliar words and chunk them, or break them into smaller parts. This helps them attack words and figure out how to read them and what they mean. When readers use chunking, they are sometimes looking at the letters in words. Sometimes, they are looking at the syllables that make up words. Other times, they are looking at prefixes, suffixes, and other word parts. Typically, skilled readers are doing all three. Knowing how to break down words is important for growing as a reader and developing fluency. Second graders encounter an increasing number of longer words in their school day. Having good word attack skills is essential.

## TYPES OF SYLLABLES

| CLOSED | OPEN | MAGIC E | VOWEL TEAM | R-CONTROLLED | CONSONANT + LE |
|---|---|---|---|---|---|
| hat<br>rab-bit | me<br>ba-by | time<br>rep-tile | coat<br>rac-coon | farm<br>mar-ket | cas-tle<br>ap-ple |
| Consonant is after the vowel. | Vowel is at the end of the syllable. | Has the vowel-consonant-silent *e* pattern. | Has two or more vowel letters together. | Vowel is followed by the letter *r*. | Has consonant and *le* at the end of a word. |
| short vowel sound | long vowel sound | long vowel sound | long, short, or special sound | /ar/, /or/, /ur/ | consonant + /l/ sound |

## BREAKING DOWN A WORD

**Compound Word:** Is it made of two smaller words? Draw a line between them.

**Suffix (Ending):** Does it end in *-ed, -ing, -ful, -tion*, etc.? Draw a line before the suffix.

**Prefix (Beginning):** Does it begin with *pre-, un-, dis-*, etc.? Draw a line after the prefix.

**Double Letters:** Do double consonants come between two vowels? Draw a line between the double consonants.

**V-C-C-V:** Are there two consonants (that don't make one sound together) between two vowels? Draw a line between the two consonants.

**V-C-V:** Is there one consonant between two vowels? Or a consonant team between two vowels?

-Try drawing a line after the first vowel. That makes the first syllable open and the vowel long. Is that a word? If not, try the first vowel as short *e*. Is that a word?

-Try drawing a line after the consonant or consonant team. That makes the first syllable closed and the vowel short. Is that a word?

# ACTIVITIES FOR BUILDING WORD ATTACK SKILLS

## CHALLENGE

Get a list of two-, three-, and four-syllable words. Use a timer to see who is the fastest at using their syllable, chunking, and phonics skills to read the words.

## Make the Word

Get a list of two-syllable words. Write each syllable on a separate index card. Each word will have one card for the first syllable and one card for the second syllable. Mix up all the cards and place them facedown. The first player flips over two cards. If they make a word, the player keeps the cards and goes again. If the cards do not make a word, the player flips them back over and the next player tries to make a match. Keep going until all cards have a match. The person with the most words wins.

## SYLLABLE HUNT

Choose one type of syllable (for example, closed syllables) or one strategy for breaking down a word (for example, dividing between double consonants). Search in books for words that have that type of syllable or that work with that dividing strategy. Write them in a list. How many can you find?

## VIDEO TEACHER

Work with your child to create a short video that teaches others how to use the syllable rules to break large words into parts. With your child's approval, share it with your child's teacher.

# FLUENCY: READING WITH EASE

Fluency is the ability to read with reasonable speed and expression. A fluent reader doesn't have to stop to decode each word. They can focus on what the story or text means. Fluency is the bridge between decoding words and comprehension.

Your second grader is beginning to read smoothly. When they read aloud, their tone and expression change to match the meaning of the text and to respond to what is happening in the story. Most second graders begin the school year reading about 50 to 60 words per minute. The goal is to read 90 words per minute by the end of the year. The best way to increase this speed is to practice, practice, practice.

### RECORD IT

After your child practices reading a book, make an audio or video recording of them reading the book aloud. Play it back. Discuss what went well and what to improve on. If your child desires, record again.

## FINDING BOOKS THAT ARE JUST RIGHT

# ACTIVITIES FOR BUILDING FLUENCY

## BOOK OF THE WEEK CHALLENGE

Choose a book that has about 50 to 80 words. It is okay if the words or sentences repeat. On Sunday, read the book together at least once. Set a timer and have your child read it aloud. Record the time it takes your child to read. Note if your child needed help. Read the same book on Monday. Time your child again and note if help was needed. Continue the process every day for a week. At the end, show your child the evidence of how they are improving in fluency.

## ECHO READING

Choose a favorite book on your child's reading level. You read the first sentence as your child slides a finger along the words. Have your child echo the first sentence as you slide your finger along the words. Then, you read the next sentence as your child slides a finger. Your child will echo the second sentence as you slide your finger. Continue the process until you have read the whole book. Remember to change your voice to respond to what is happening in the story. Encourage your child to change their voice, too.

### TOO EASY

- You know all the words.
- You can easily retell the story.
- You have read the book many times before.
- You are reading too fast.

Does this describe your book? Try a more difficult book.

### JUST RIGHT

- You know most of the words.
- You understand what you are reading, and you can retell it.
- You are reading at a steady pace.

Does this describe your book? This book is just right for you!

### TOO HARD

- There are lots of tricky words.
- You forget important information as you read.
- You are reading too slowly.

Does this describe your book? Try an easier book.

# VOCABULARY:
# WORDS HAVE MEANING

Vocabulary plays a critical role in the process of learning to read. Young readers use their knowledge about words to make sense of what they are reading. In order to understand what is read, a child must know what the words mean. Children need a large mental "word bank" to draw on as they read. The larger a child's vocabulary, the more they are able to comprehend what they are reading or listening to.

As new words are encountered, children link them to words they already know to add to their growing vocabularies. Some words are learned naturally. Others must be taught. Children learn new words through daily conversations and by having experiences that teach them about the world. Reading books to your child also exposes them to rich language.

## MAP IT!

Create a thinking map. Write a vocabulary word in the center of a sheet of paper. Then, divide the paper into four sections. In the first box, write a simple definition. In the second box, write examples or words that mean the same as the vocabulary word. In the third box, make a connection to something in your life or something you know. In the fourth box, add a picture that represents the word.

| Definition<br>to get the same kinds of things and keep them | Examples/Synonyms<br>gather<br>save |
| --- | --- |
| Connection<br>I collect stuffies. | Picture<br> |

Center word: collect

## TYPES OF VOCABULARY

**Listening Vocabulary:** The words we hear
**Speaking Vocabulary:** The words we say
**Reading Vocabulary:** The words we read
**Writing Vocabulary:** The words we use to write

# ACTIVITIES FOR BUILDING VOCABULARY

## WORDS FROM NONFICTION

Choose a nonfiction book. Read the book aloud to your child. Talk about new words from the book. Have your child share with others the new words they learned.

## NEW WORD TALK

Introduce a new word to your child by providing a simple definition. Then, give an example that relates to your child's experiences. Have your child think of an example, too. Over the next few days, take the opportunity to use the new word in conversation.

## NEW WORDS WHILE READING

When your child is reading, it is okay to stop to discuss a new word. Reread the sentence and ask what your child thinks the new word means. Give a child-friendly definition. Help your child make a personal connection to the word.

## MY VOCABULARY JOURNAL

Have your child keep a vocabulary journal. Use a spiral-bound notebook or composition book. Write one vocabulary word on each page. Draw a picture that represents the word. Write a kid-friendly definition. Write a sentence that uses the word.

# COMPREHENSION: UNDERSTANDING WHAT IS READ

Reading comprehension is the essence of reading. It is the ability to gain meaning from what you read. This is a complex skill that develops over time. Children can begin growing in this area by taking time to think about what they have just read. As children read, their minds must be "turned on" and thinking actively about what they are reading.

Second graders should be able to understand books they read and books that are read to them. They can answer questions about a story. They can find evidence by looking through the book. For fiction books, they can tell about the characters, setting, and important events. For nonfiction books, they can give important facts from the book.

| | |
|---|---|
|  | Funny part |
|  | Important part |
|  | Surprising or shocking part |
|  | Confusing part or unknown word |
|  | Part where I made a connection |
| 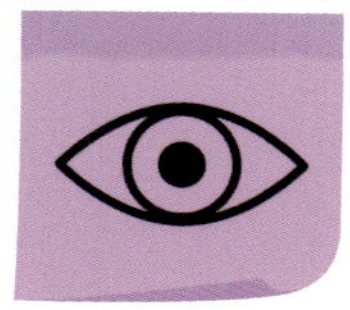 | Part where I visualized something |
|  | Part where I predicted something |
|  | Part where I understood something |

## ACTIVE READING

Active reading happens when the reader is involved and engaged with the text. The reader is thinking about what is being read and making connections. This type of reading is essential for comprehension.

Help your child practice active reading by drawing symbols on sticky notes to show their thinking as they read. Use the examples above.

# ACTIVITIES FOR BUILDING READING COMPREHENSION

## SHARED READING

Choose a book. Read aloud the first paragraph or first couple of sentences. Talk about what was read. Have your child read the next paragraph or couple of sentences. Continue to discuss the story as you share the reading.

## MAKE A NOTE (NONFICTION BOOKS)

Fold a sheet of paper into fourths. In the center of the paper, write the main topic of the book. Then, in each section, write and illustrate a fact about the topic.

## BEGINNING-MIDDLE-END (FICTION BOOKS)

Fold a sheet of paper into thirds. In the first section, draw and label a picture of what happened in the beginning of the story. In the second section, draw and label a picture of what happened in the middle. In the third section, draw and label a picture of what happened at the end of the story. Use the drawings to talk about and retell the story.

## COMPREHENSION QUESTIONS

**For Nonfiction (Real-World) Books**

**Before Reading**

- What is the title? What clues does the title give about the book?
- What do you think you will learn by reading this book?

**During Reading**

- Are there any bold words? Why? What information does this add?
- How do the pictures and captions help you understand the words?

**After Reading**

- What is the book mainly about? Why is this topic important?
- What did you find most interesting about the topic?
- How did the author make it easy to find information (through headings, charts, etc.)?

**For Fiction Books**

**Before Reading**

- Who is the author? Who is the illustrator? What do they do?
- What do you think will happen in the story?

**During Reading**

- What do you think will happen next? How do you think the character will react?
- How do the illustrations explain what is happening in the story?

**After Reading**

- What was the problem in the story? How was the problem solved?
- What is the setting of the story? Where did the story take place?
- How does the main character change from the beginning to the end?

# WRITING: SHOWING UNDERSTANDING

Children are often asked to write about what they read. They also write to tell about their own ideas. When children write, they show their understanding of phonics, high-frequency words, vocabulary, and more. They demonstrate that they have internalized what they have learned and made it their own.

Second graders take pride in their growing ability to express their ideas through writing. Their handwriting is becoming more legible. They can write multiple sentences about the same topic. They expand, revise, and check their own work. Second grade writers are beginning to remember to use capital letters and punctuation marks. Their spelling is becoming more accurate.

## WHEN WRITING IS HARD

- Use a text-to-speech feature on a computer. Then, have your child copy on paper.
- Use a thinking map. Write the topic in a box at the top of a sheet of paper. Underneath, draw three smaller boxes. Write or draw one detail or example in each small box. Use the map to help write a paragraph.
- Have your child tell you what to write. Help them create the sentences. When you are finished, your child can copy what you wrote.
- When your child starts writing, set a timer for 10 minutes. When the timer goes off, take a 10-minute break. Continue this pattern until the writing is complete.

## DON'T FORGET YOUR CAPS!

**C**apitalization
**A**ll sentences make sense
**P**unctuation
**S**pelling/Spacing

# ACTIVITIES FOR BUILDING WRITING SKILLS

## TELL ME HOW

Have your child choose an everyday task like making the bed or washing your hands. Ask your child to write step-by-step instructions. Then, you read the steps and follow them exactly. Have your child edit the instructions to make them clearer. Then, switch roles.

## POPPING WORDS

*Good, big, nice.* Some words are generic and don't make writing come alive. In a journal, write a generic word at the top of a page. Below, write more descriptive words that could replace it. As you find more words that add "pop" to your writing, add them to the journal. Use these examples.

good: *excellent, delightful, amazing*

big: *huge, gigantic, enormous*

nice: *kind, thoughtful, gracious*

## SENTENCE STRETCH

Have your child write a sentence with three to five words. Write each word on a sticky note or index card and place them in front of your child. Then, ask your child to think of words to add to the sentence to make it longer. Make a sticky note or card for each new word. How long can your child make the sentence?

The pig ate.

The pig ate ice cream.

The pink pig ate rocky road ice cream.

The pink pig with orange spots ate rocky road ice cream.

The pink pig with orange spots ate rocky road ice cream at the park.

# WRITING:
# HAVING A PURPOSE

Second graders write for a variety of purposes. They write to tell stories about personal experiences and the experiences of fictional characters. They write reports to explain facts. They write letters that persuade others to agree with their opinions. Writers at this age are learning to think about who will read what they write and how to make sure that their writing speaks to their specific audience.

Second graders can organize their writing to match its purpose. They can put sentences together in a logical order. They write stories that have a clear beginning, middle, and end. They write paragraphs that include a main idea or topic sentence, sentences that provide details and examples, and a closing or ending sentence.

### TYPES OF WRITING

**Narrative Writing:** Tells a story

**Informative Writing:** Gives information

**Opinion Writing:** Gives an opinion

## HOW TO WRITE A PARAGRAPH

A paragraph that gives information or expresses an opinion can be written with five sentences. The first sentence is the main idea or topic sentence that tells what the paragraph is going to explain. The next three sentences contain details or examples that support, prove, or explain the main idea. The fifth and last sentence closes up or ends the paragraph. Children can use the fingers on their hands to remind them of the parts needed for a good paragraph.

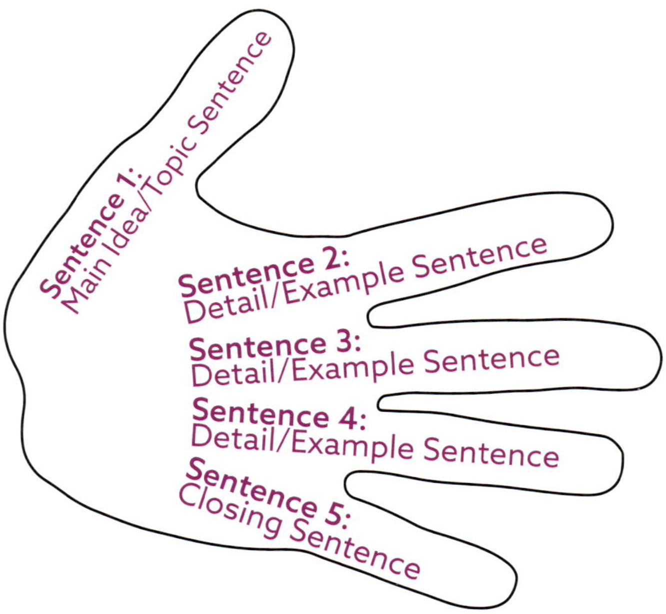

# ACTIVITIES FOR BUILDING WRITING SKILLS

## IN MY OPINION...

Under your supervision, help your child write and submit an online review of a book, a movie, a product, or a recipe they have tried. Encourage your child to practice writing a persuasive opinion by providing reasons, evidence, and examples to support their conclusions.

## FAMILY STORIES

Encourage your child to learn your family's history by talking to you and to other relatives about stories from the past. What sport did Grandpa play when he was young? What happened to Aunt Rose on a camping trip? Your child can listen to lots of stories and then choose a favorite to write and illustrate. Publish the story by sharing it with family members.

## KEEP A JOURNAL

Encourage your child to keep a writing journal. It can include diary entries, questions, drawings, ideas, and lists. Occasionally, provide prompts for journal entries. For example, say, "Write about what you would like to do this summer" or "Write something you wonder about."

## PICTURE PROMPT

Help your child search online for an interesting photograph. It could show an animal, a place on Earth, an invention, a person from history, or something else. Encourage your child to research the subject of the photo and to write a short report to tell facts they learned.

# SPELLING: USING THE CODE

When children sound out a word, they use their knowledge of the phonics code to decode it. By contrast, when they spell a word, they use their knowledge of the phonics code to encode it. They must match a letter or group of letters to each sound heard in a word. Children can usually read words before they can spell them. But practicing spelling improves reading ability. Good spellers are generally good readers, and vice versa.

In second grade, students practice spelling words that follow phonics rules. They also spell frequently-used words that don't follow phonics rules. By the end of the school year, second graders are expected to spell words with short vowels, words with long vowels, words in which the vowel letter is followed by the letter *r*, and words with consonant blends. Compound words such as *sandbox* are also introduced.

## LEARNING TO SPELL RULE-BREAKERS

Many English words do not follow phonics rules. But it is still important for children to know how to spell them. Try these strategies.

**Say, Spell and Write, Read and Underline:** Say the word. Write the word while saying the name of each letter. Underline the word from left to right as you read it. Repeat five times in a row.

**Triangle Word:** Say the word. Write the first letter. Say the word. Write the first two letters. Say the word. Write the first three letters. Continue the pattern until the word is written. Then, say the word and write the full word three more times. See the example at right.

d
do
doe
does
does
does
does

**Trace It:** Write the word and read it. Trace each letter with your finger as you say its name. Use your finger to swipe under the word from left to right as you read it. Repeat three times. Then, close your eyes and use your finger to write each letter of the word in the air.

**Chunk It:** Break a longer word into syllables or groups of letters. Say the word. Write each chunk, saying the names of the letters as you write them. Pause after each chunk. Read the word. Repeat three times.

**second:** sec-ond OR se-co-nd

# ACTIVITIES FOR BUILDING SPELLING SKILLS

## NOTICE PATTERNS

Have your child look at a group of words and note any patterns. For example, "I see that when long *a* is at the end of a word, it is spelled *ay*." Study these words together.

## SPOT IT

Write two lists of words side-by-side so that each word pair shows a word spelled correctly and incorrectly. Have your child find the correctly spelled words.

## ROLL IT

Prepare a set of 20 word cards for each player. Choose words that match each child's grade level. Use sight words, words from the child's previous spelling lists, or grade-level words found online. Stack the cards in each set and place them facedown. The first player rolls a die and draws the matching number of cards from their stack of words. (If a 4 is rolled, they pick up 4 cards.) Have a helper read each word aloud as the player spells it. The player gets to keep the card for each word spelled correctly. For incorrect responses, the card goes back in the stack. Take turns rolling, drawing cards, and spelling. The first player with 10 cards is the winner.

## DO I USE C OR K?

When writing a word that begins with the /k/ sound, how do you know which letter to use? It depends on which vowel letter follows it. This rhyme will help: *C* goes with *a*, *o*, and *u*, and *k* goes with the other two (*e*, *i*). Try it with words such as *kind*, *cute*, *catch*, and *key*.

*C* goes with *a*, *o*, and *u*.

*K* goes with the other two.

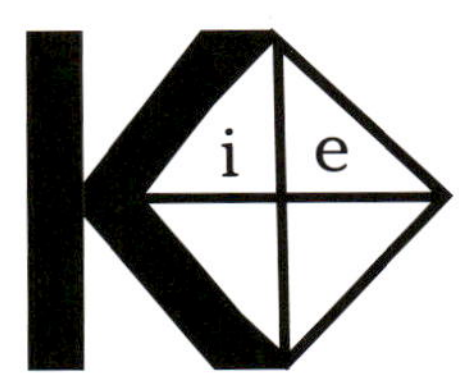

# WHAT TO DO WHEN YOUR CHILD STRUGGLES

As a parent, it is frustrating when your child has difficulties. When this happens, it is important to seek out help. Begin with your child's classroom teacher, who might be able to provide more personalized instruction and strategies to try at home. You can also reach out to a reading specialist or special education teacher at your school or district. Tutors, professionals in private practice, and reading clinics are other ways to support your child.

If your child continues to struggle, ask the school to have a meeting that includes the classroom teacher, reading or literacy coach, school psychologist, school counselor, and special education teacher. This is an opportunity for everyone to be honest and open in a supportive way. The goal of such a meeting is to gather information in order to decide how to move forward. Some possible outcomes are formal evaluation for special education, creation of a 504 Plan or Individualized Education Plan (IEP), more intensive instruction by the classroom teacher, or referral to a pediatrician for a possible medical diagnosis.

## QUESTIONS FOR TEAM DISCUSSION

- Are there attention issues at school? At home?
- Is poor attendance having an impact?
- When were the child's hearing and vision last checked?
- Does the child speak another language?
- Did the child struggle with reading in previous grades?
- What supports and strategies have been in place? Were they successful?
- Does the child have a medical condition that may impact learning?

# HOW TO HELP AT HOME

If your child is reading below grade level, you'll want to enlist the support of their classroom teacher and other experts. However, you have an important role to play. Your encouragement can make a big difference when it comes to your child's attitude about reading, motivation to read, and steady growth as a reader. Try these suggestions.

## 1. NOTICE STUMBLING BLOCKS

Not all reading problems are alike. You are in a unique position to notice when and why your child is struggling. Read with your child and take note of what is challenging. Then you'll be able to make a plan for getting help. Some reasons for concern are avoidance of reading, slow and labored oral reading, and having trouble with books well below grade level. Share specific observations and concerns with your child's teachers.

## 2. KEEP READING

Make reading every day a joyful part of your home. Make sure your child has easy access to a variety of reading materials. Let your child see you reading for pleasure and for finding information. Talk about what you are reading and encourage your child to talk about what they are reading. This will lead to rich conversations that help your child build vocabulary and language skills.

## 3. FIND THE RIGHT BOOKS

Let your child choose books that interest them. Seek out books that relate to your child's interests. Reading books in a series is a good way to encourage reading comprehension as children become familiar with different stories about the same characters. Graphic novels and early chapter books can help children bridge from picture books and read-alouds into more independent reading.

## 4. HAVE FUN

Sometimes, children get the message that reading is a chore. Make it fun by encouraging your child to draw pictures and write stories about favorite characters, act out stories, and take turns reading aloud with you or with a sibling. By joining in the fun, your child will steadily build skills and grow as a reader.

# WORDS TO KNOW

**504 Plan:** a plan that describes the accommodations that the school will provide to support the student's education

**active reading:** when a reader is thinking about, involved with, and engaged in a text

**decoding:** the ability to sound out written words

**ELA:** English language arts

**ELL:** English language learner

**ESE:** exceptional student education

**fluency:** the ability to read with speed, accuracy, and appropriate expression

**high-frequency word:** a word that often appears in written material and that can be decoded using common phonics rules

**IEP:** individualized education plan; a personalized plan that describes the special education instruction, supports, and services a child needs

**Lexile level:** a scientific measurement of the complexity and readability of a text

**literacy:** the ability to read and write

**phonemic awareness:** the ability to identify and manipulate individual sounds in spoken words

**phonics:** matching the sounds of spoken English to individual letters or groups of letters; the relationship between sounds and letters

**phonological awareness:** the ability to identify and manipulate syllables and other parts of spoken words